WHAT DIVIDES US & HOW TO DEFEAT TRUMP IN 2020

By Willard Bumblebee

I0419624

The budget deficit for fiscal year
currently outpacing prior years

Federal Budget Deficit (Billions of Dollars)

2016   2017   2018   2019

Dec   Jan   Feb   Mar   Apr   May   Jun

ury, *Monthly Treasury Statement*, issues for September 2015 through Ji
ns on October 1 and ends on September 30; it is designated by the calend
ion

MIGRATION

VOTE

NOT YOURS TO RECLAIM

STOP RACISM NOW

NEVER AGAIN
ABORTION RIGHTS NOW
DEFEND WOMEN'S HEALTH

GUNS RIGHTS VERSUS GUN CONTROL

The 2nd Amendment

A well regulated militia, being necessary to the security of a free state, the right of the people to keep and bear arms, shall not be infringed.

The 2nd Amendment is one of the most divisive issues in the country today. Republicans want very little regulations, rules or laws around gun ownership while Democrats want to regulate or limit access to firearms to prevent some of the mass killings due to gun violence.

Why should American citizens have the right to own a semi-Automatic assault rifle, a weapon of war? The sole purpose of such guns is to kill as many people as possible. They are not used for home(self) protection or hunting. These guns are often the weapon of choice for many mass shooters. So, it is a valid question to ask why such guns should be sold to ordinary citizens. Many industrialized nations have taken steps to reduce gun violence after mass shootings and the gun control laws implemented have kept those countries from experiencing the same mass killings again and again like what we see in the United States.

After shooting incidents in 1996 & 1997, Australia enacted very strict gun laws to make sure that tragedies like that never happen again. They took actions to prevent those types of shootings from happening.

After the Christchurch mosque shootings in New Zealand in 2019, the parliament passed 119 to 1 to restrict semi-automatic firearms and provide a buyback of these weapons. They took an important step for the good of their country, to make sure that tragedies like that never happen again.

After the Sandy Hook Elementary School shooting that happened on December 14, 2012, in Newtown, Connecticut, when a disturbed 20-year-old Adam Lanza shot and killed 26 people, including 20 kids between six and seven years old, and six adult members of staff, I thought Republicans would put politics aside and join Democrats to make sure disturbed individuals like Adam Lanza never have access to such firearms again.

*CNN news coverage of the **Sandy Hook Elementary School shooting** that happened on December 14, 2012, in Newtown, Connecticut*

I was dead wrong. Republicans blocked all efforts to such measures. For a party that says that it is a pro-life party, the Republicans really do not care about life once a baby is born. They are simply a pro-birth party not a pro-life party. They could not act after 20 kids were gunned down while attending school. There have been countless mass shootings since then at schools, churches, malls, concerts and the workplace.

According to the news, On August 3rd, 2019 in El Paso, Texas, a 21-year-old Trump supporter killed 20 and injured 26 at a Walmart shopping center. Just 13 hours later a 24-year-old gunman in Dayton, Ohio used an assault style rifle to kill 9 people and injure 27 others in popular night club district.

Sensible gun laws that protect American citizens right to life should not be a partisan issue, it should be a duty of law makers. The National Rifle Association (NRA) has so much political power and it opposes any gun control measures even in the case of preventing those on the 'do not fly' list from owning guns. Their political power comes from pouring money into the campaigns of pro-gun politicians that help them win elections and money against gun control politicians. In the Republican party, being a gun control politician can often mean the end of a career.

The NRA is in the business of selling as many guns as possible and making as much money as possible without any regard to the right to life.

Unless the voters start voting in politicians that have the guts to introduce gun reform legislation while still preserving guns rights and a President that would sign it, these tragedies will continue to happen. The main reason that this has not happened is because the Republicans have blocked gun control measures and they have been largely rewarded for it by continuing to win elections. Gun right voters are often single-issue voters while control gun voters do not vote on that single issue. That needs to change. We are currently a nation of gun care and health control. It is a shame!

Ruger AR-556 5.56mm Semi-Auto Rifle. A semi-automatic gun, a weapon of choice for most mass shooters

HEALTH CARE

The Republican party has spent the last decade trying to take away healthcare from millions and millions of Americans and it has not been a secret. The reason private health insurance is so expensive is because the republican party has blocked every single effort by the democrats to improve health care in the country. Instead of working with Democrats to improve the law in helping to bring down cost, they voted 50+ times in the house to repeal the law during president Obama's presidency with no viable replacement.

Several Republican state governments and the trump administration are in court now suing to have the entire Affordable Care Act (Obamacare) scrapped.

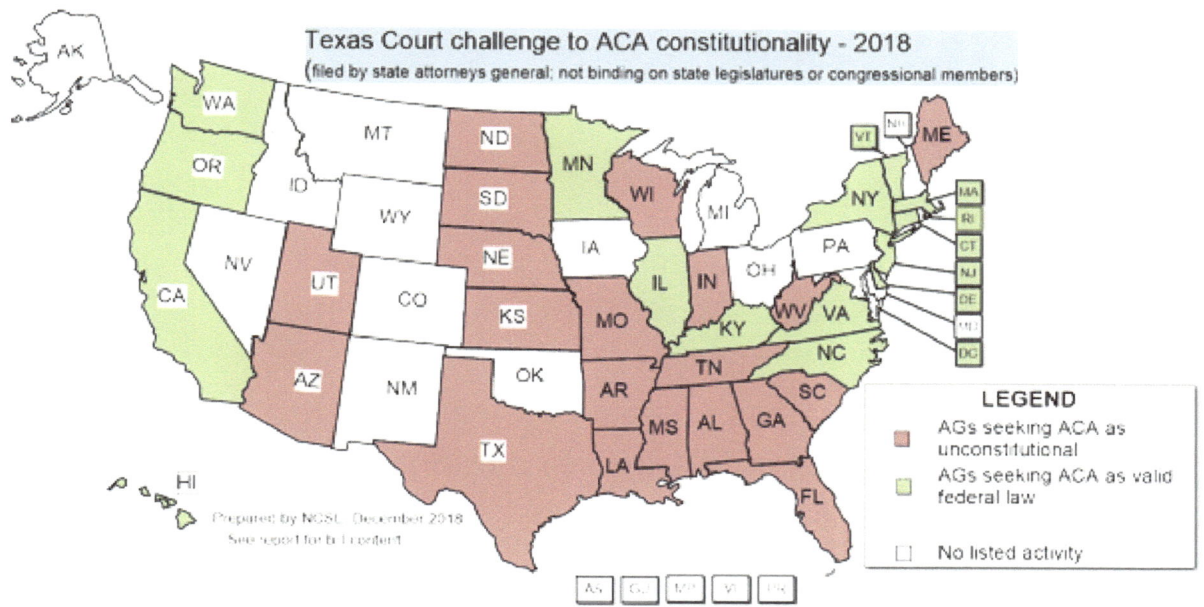

Photo from National Conference of State Legislatures

They could not do it through the legislative process so now they are trying to kill the law through the courts. What that means is that the pre-existing protections that the healthcare law provides (insurance companies cannot not deny individuals coverage due to a pre-existing condition) would be completely abandoned. Republicans have no viable replacement. That means millions could be left without health insurance coverage. Most of those that would be affected are die hard Republicans.

The Republican party has also openly talked about cutting Medicare(Medicare is a federal health insurance program for people who are 65 or older, certain younger people with disabilities, people with End-Stage Renal Disease), Medicaid(a federal and state program that helps with medical costs for people with low or limited income) and Social Security(a federal insurance program that provides income to retired people and those who are unemployed or disabled). It is not a secret. After giving large profitable companies huge tax cuts, the republicans are now trying to reduce the growing budget deficit on the backs of senior citizens.

The white working class seems to ignore all these policies that Republicans aspire to pass that would hurt them, if their elected politicians engage in divisive racial resentment politics. The white working class are told that these programs, especially Medicaid benefit minorities and immigrants. If immigrants and minorities do not have access, they seem to be fine with losing those benefits as well.

Of the 10 poorest states in the country, only New Mexico is a blue state. The rest: West Virginia, Mississippi, Arkansas, Louisiana, Alabama, Kentucky, Oklahoma, South Carolina, and Tennessee are all red states. These states are also the least healthy states that rely on federal and state programs for healthcare and sustenance. Voters in these states vote against their interest when they continue to support a party that seeks to cut, eliminate or deny them access to these programs.

It is time the Republicans get called out on their hypocrisy. Medicare, Medicaid and Social Security were passed by progressives and liberals with massive opposition by conservatives. They would rather cut taxes for wealthy individuals and profitable wealthy corporations than to provide affordable access to health insurance for even their constituents. They are perfectly fine with socialism if it is a giveaway to the rich and wealthy corporations. They get away with bad policies because their base is more focused on racial resentment politics which the Republican politicians are happy to use as a red meat issue time and time again. The Republican party is a flat-out majority racist party.

It used to be a conservative party with a racist fringe. Now under Donald trump, it is a white nationalist party with a conservative fringe.

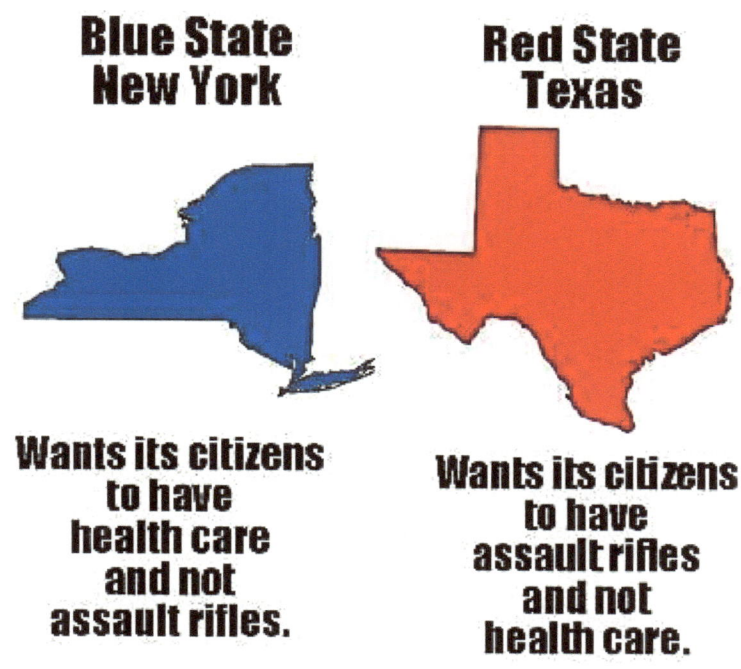

Blue State New York

Wants its citizens to have health care and not assault rifles.

Red State Texas

Wants its citizens to have assault rifles and not health care.

ABORTION

Being pro-choice does not mean that you are pro- abortion. It just means that you believe that a woman and her doctor have the right to make the difficult health care decision on what is right for the woman.

The Republican politicians use this as a divisive issue to win support from the extreme religious right. They gin up support from creating fake stories about late term abortions which are already illegal in all states.

Some Republican states have moved to criminalize abortion even in the case of rape and incent event as Roe V Wade (legal case in which the U.S. Supreme Court on January 22, 1973, ruled 7–2 that unduly restrictive state regulation of abortion is unconstitutional) is still the law of the land. **An example of that is the Human Life Protection Act signed into law by Governor Kay Ivey on May 19th, 2019.** Under the Alabama law, a medical professional who performs a banned abortion in the state of Alabama would be guilty of a Class A felony and could be sentenced to life imprisonment.

Protesters for women's rights march to the Alabama Capitol to protest a law passed last week making abortion a felony in nearly all cases with no exceptions for cases of rape or incest, Sunday, May 19, 2019, in Montgomery, Ala. (AP Photo/Butch Dill)

The Republican party is the only party in the developed world that still has this issue around abortion rights. The party is basically a pro-birth party, not a pro-life party because they could care less about what happens to that child once that child is born. They have advocated cutting safety net programs that help low income families with kids such as the Supplemental Nutrition Assistance Program (SNAP), commonly known as the Food Stamp Program, which provides food-purchasing assistance for low- and no-income people living in the United States.

They did not care enough to pass legislation that would prevent loss of life due to gun violence such as the sandy hook massacre where 20 innocent kids lost their lives by simply attending school.

CLIMATE CHANGE

What South Beach, Miami, would probably look like if temperatures rise by 2 degrees Celsius. Image courtesy of Nickolay Lamm/ClimateCentral/sealevel.climatecentral.org

Every day we see the signs of extreme weather: Flooding, tornados, hurricanes, very hot and humid temperatures and yet the Republican party, the only major political party in the developed world denies that climate change is happening.

One of the first things that Donald Trump did as President was remove the U.S from the Paris Climate change accord which was negotiated by the Obama administration to combat climate change around the world. Nearly every country in the world had signed on to take steps to fight climate change and protect the planet for future generations. Talk about American leadership to get nearly all the countries in the world including China and Russia to agree to fight climate change. With a stroke of a pen, Trump took all that progress away.

The main reason Trump did this is because it was negotiated by Obama whom he hates and whose legacy he wants to decimate. The Trump administration has reversed several Obama era regulations meant at protecting the environment. The Environmental Protection Agency (EPA) under Trump has been riddled with corruption and controversy and has led the way in climate change science denial. According to an Associated Press report, Scott Pruitt (Trump's EPA Chief) faces "more than a dozen allegations that [he] has misused his office to obtain perks and material benefits for himself and his family, including costly, taxpayer-funded premium-class trips and round-the-clock security." He resigned on July 5th, 2018.

RACE RELATIONS

Under Donald Trump, race relations have gotten extremely worse. Hate crimes are significantly up during his presidency. Most recently On August 3rd, 2019, a white Nationalist shot and Killed 20 people at a Walmart in El Paso, TX and wounded 26 others. On his manifesto online he indicated he wanted to kill Mexicans because he believed they were 'invading' the country, a term Trump as used before.

Trump is a racist that has said many racist things. He began his announcement as a candidate for President by calling Mexicans, drug dealers and rapists. He has given cover to hate groups by equating white supremacists with those protesting hate in Charlottesville, VA in 2017 by saying 'there were fine people on both sides' He is the founder of the 'birther' movement against America's first African American President by spreading lies that President Obama was born in Kenya and therefore was ineligible to have been elected President.

He has called mostly African American athletes who had knelt down during the national anthem as a protest to racial injustice 'sons of bitches' He has referred to African Countries as 'Shithole' Countries.

Recently he twitted that 4 duly elected congress women of color go back to their countries. 3 of them were born in this country (Alexandria Ocasio-Cortez, D-NY, Rashida Tlaib D-MI, Ayanna Pressley D-MA). Ilhan Omar is an immigrant from Somalia who has been a naturalized US citizen since the year 2000, 5 years after she entered the country as a Somalia refugee. There have been countless other times where Trump has twitted racist dog whistle language and has refused to denounce racism time and time again.

"If you can convince the lowest white man he's better than the best colored man, he won't notice you're picking his pocket. Hell, give him somebody to look down on, and he'll empty his pockets for you." — **Lyndon B. Johnson**

One common lie that the Republicans like to put out there is that Republicans freed the slaves and thereby the party cannot be racist. The ones that push this fallacy say it like they believe it so let me set the record straight. It is true that Republicans freed the slaves but the republican party that did that was made of progressives and liberals while the Democrat party that opposed it was full of southern conservatives. The parties switched ideologies. Once the Democrats started focusing on civil rights in the 60's, the southerners fled the Democrat party and have been Republicans since. It is accurate to say progressives and liberals who make up the Democrat party today freed the slaves not the conservatives or southerners that make up the republican party today.

The reason why Donald Trump is President today is because African Americans sat out the 2016 elections. The Trump campaign along with the Russians did a good job in suppressing turnout by portraying Hillary Clinton as a terrible person that probably committed crimes with her email server. There is no excuse this time. If African Americans and young people turn out to vote in high levels, no matter who the Democrats nominate for President is, Trump is going to lose the blue wall states he carried narrowly, MI, WI, PA and thereby the election. There is no time for complacency. Another 4 years of Donald Trump would be a disaster for the country and the world. If you think Donald Trump is bad now, wait till you see what happens with a Donald Trump that does not have to seek re-election. Vote!

If you can wait 5 hours in line on black Friday for the latest iPhone or Nike sneakers, you can take 30 minutes out of your day to vote every 2 years.

You would not let your Grandparents pick your clothes for you, why would you let them pick your President, senators or representatives. Countless people fought and died to give every single US citizen the right to vote. Honor them, Vote!

SUPREME COURT

Under President Trump the supreme court has become too political. Mitch McConnell's main goal as the Senate Majority leader is to pack the courts with far-right activist judges for generations to come to thwart a Democrat President's agenda. He does not care about the constitution.

McConnell was able to block President Obama's Supreme court nominee, Merrick Garland for almost a year after the passing of Justice Antonin Scalia in 2016. McConnell is from a poor state of Kentucky. He had the power to block a president who was elected by at least 51% of the popular vote twice because democrats only care to vote in presidential elections, and many do not even turn out to vote then. Elections have consequences. McConnell became the senate majority leader after the 2014 mid-term elections when only 36.6% of eligible voters turned out to vote. Low turnout favors republicans. Elections have consequences. Vote!

Trump who won just 46% of the popular vote has been able to pick two far right supreme court Justices who get to decide the lives of every single person in this country. After blocking President Obama's supreme court nominee, McConnell changed the rules in the senate from a 60-senate vote threshold to just a simple majority to confirm supreme court justices. This has never been done before because the court is meant to be above politics. The will of the American people is under assault by Moscow Mitch.

Elections has consequences folks and the senate elections are just as important if not more important that presidential elections. If Mitch McConnell remains the senate majority leader, it does not matter if there is a Democrat President, nothing significant is going to get done. He is going to obstruct court nominees and thwart the Democrat

President's agenda. Republicans understood what was at stake in the 2016 election while democrats remained complacent and divided. This cannot happen again. Please vote!

It is the duty of every Democrat elected official to emphasis the importance of winning the presidency, senate and keeping the house. If they do not win the senate and presidency, Trump will have two more supreme court justices on the bench that will change the face of the nation for generations. Democrats need to emphasis the importance of the courts in their bid to take control of all branches of government.

Left: Brett Kavanaugh, Right: Neil Gorsuch. Both are Supreme court Justices picked by Donald Trump

IMMIGRATION

The Republican party politicians do not want to do anything about immigration because they want to continue to use it as a campaign issue to continue to get elected. The base is very opposed to any compromise on immigration.

In 2013 during the Obama Presidency, the senate passed a bipartisan comprehensive immigration by a 68-32 margin. It was a bill that would have increased border security by adding up to 40,000 border patrol agents, double boarder fencing and was designed to stop 90% of illegal immigration. That bill passed with 68 votes in the senate. That is extremely unlikely in today's hyper partisan climate. Jon Boehner, the then Republican speaker of the house refused to bring the bill up for a vote. That bill did not become law because the Republican speaker did not allow the house of representations to vote on it. Had they had the opportunity to vote for it, that bill would have become law. That bill would have modernized immigration enforcement and prevent most of the problems at the border today.

We have a President now that has committed human rights violation at the border by kidnapping kids from their parents and locking them up in cages with inadequate food, clothing and personal care items.

Donald trump shut down the government for 35 days (longest government shutdown in history) to force congress to provide funds for a border wall, 8 times less than the amount in the 2013 immigration bill under Obama. All he cares about is proving to his base that he is fighting to build a wall that he said Mexico was going to pay for. Trump lost the government shut down fight so he went around congress and declared a national emergency at the boarder which would allow him to steal 2 billion dollars from the military defense fund to build the wall. Talk about not giving a damn about the constitution which gives congress the power of purse.

Republicans have portrayed Democrats as wanting open borders, that they want more illegal immigration to get more votes, that they love immigrants more than US citizens etc. None of this is true. It is meant to gin up a base with cultural anxiety about America being a majority minority nation some 30 years in future.

Obama was called the deporter-in-chief because he enforced immigration laws without using it exclusively for political gain. Democrats have never been for open borders, but the Republicans will continue to tell that lie. It is important for every Democrat to educate the American people that their immigration policies are different from the Republicans but they are strictly opposed to open borders and that they are for more modernized border security not an ineffective wall that Trump promised Mexico was going to pay for.

Fox news will lie about the Democrats' position any second they get. No immigrant comes to America saying they are going to vote for Democrats but when they get here and see and hear the intolerance from the Republican party, they tend to lean Democrat. The Republican party should compete for every vote instead of focusing on a shrinking white working-class vote by stoking the flames of racism, xenophobia and misogyny.

CRIMINAL JUSTICE REFORM

Black people go to jail for the same crimes that white people go to rehab for. The criminal Justice system is not Equal. If the police focus on catching a certain group of people, that is all they are going to catch even when crimes are being committed right under their nose by others.

If you are rich and of any race, you tend of get off or get sweet deals for the same crime or offenses that poor people spend years in jail for. This tends to affect minorities more than whites.

Once a person is incarcerated, they tend to go on living a life of crime because the system is unforgiving and many ex-cons struggle getting a job after prison because no one wants to take a chance on an ex-convict. Many of their offenses are nonviolent drug offenses.

The U.S must move from mass incarceration to crime prevention and intervention to give more at risk individuals an opportunity to go on to live more fruitful and productive lives. The democrat candidates for president can and should discuss a vision of preventing the high school to prison pipeline.

ELECTORAL COLLEGE

For true democracy to foster, the electoral college must be eliminated. One man one vote. When a President wins the presidency, his policies affect every single person in the country so he should be required to win the majority of the vote.

It is already bad enough that small states like Wyoming with a little over 500,000 residents get the same representation as California with 40 million residents in the senate. Both states get 2 senators representing the states. It is not a fair system for modern times. Washington DC has twice the population of Wyoming and they have no senate representation. It is a travesty.

It is easier to hack an election when one only has to focus on about 5 states. With a one man one vote system, all presidential candidates will have to work for every single vote from CA to SC to VT. That will force presidential candidates to be more moderate and practical.

It is possible that Russia hacked the electoral systems in PA, MI, WI, FL and flipped the votes for Trump. No one has been willing to say that but if it is possible to hack into a server and access emails, why is it impossible to hack into electronic voter systems and manipulate the vote?! Every state should have a paper trail to audit the vote count in the event of a disputed election. That is just what Democrats are proposing for the 2020 elections, but Mitch McConnell has blocked the election security bills in the senate. Pretty much what that means is that Mitch 'Moscow' McConnell, Trump and the Republicans welcome Russia interference in the 2020 elections to get Trump elected again.

Democrats should not be willing to accept the election results if Trump wins again without election security measures but frankly, I do not think the Republicans care. They have been cheating to win elections for decades from suppressing the vote through restrictive vote ID laws, to gerrymandering to outright accepting foreign help.

The number one goal for Democrat governors in MI, WI and PA is to sign executive actions to make sure there are paper trails on every vote and that the Russians know that they cannot get away with hacking voter systems this time around

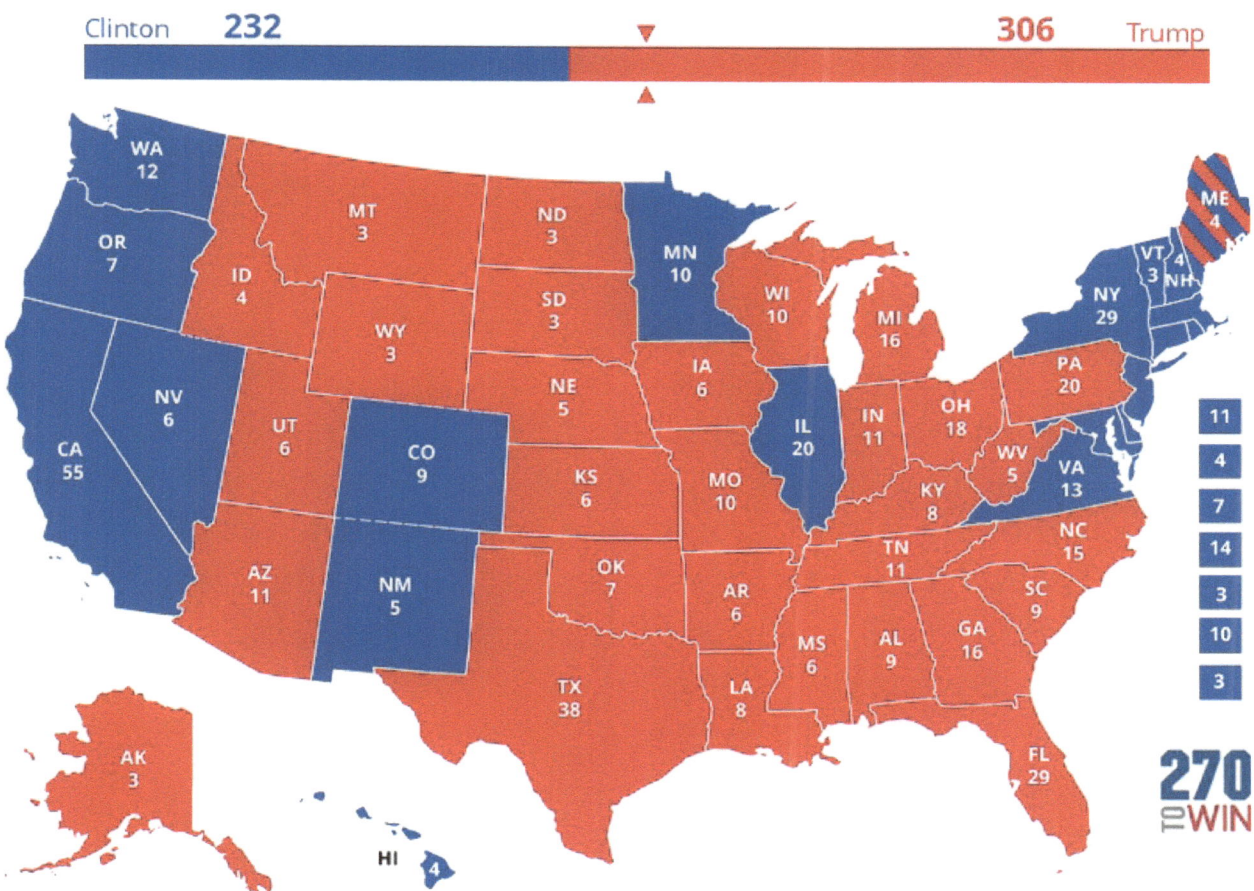

Google image of 2016 electoral college result! Trump won the presidency although Hilary Clinton won almost 3 million more votes

VOTING RIGHTS

Voting rights have been under relentless assault by the Republican party. They have gerrymandered (manipulate the boundaries of an electoral constituency to favor one party) state and congressional districts to give themselves an unfair advantage to win more elections. In states that they control, they have passed strict voter ID laws that prevent Democrat constituents from voting. Trump has tried and failed to rig the census by adding a citizenship status question which might prevent certain undocumented residents or residents of color from filling out the forms which will lead to an undercount and thus fewer federal funds and less representation in congress.

The last two Republican Presidents, George W Bush and Donald trump were elected President under suspicious circumstances while losing the popular vote.

Bush was elected after the Republican supreme court ordered vote counting to stop in the state of FL where he presumably won by about 537 votes over Al Gore. Jeb Bush, George W. Bush's younger brother was the governor of the state at that time and FL had been called earlier as a win for Gore before it was recalled after Jeb Bush stepped in. It was very suspicious. Ultimately the Republican supreme court made Bush President against the wishes of the American voters.

Trump was elected president with heavy Russian interference and possibly a hack into the voter systems. He lost nearly 3 million more votes than Hillary Clinton and lost 54 % of the popular vote. PA, WI and MI had not voted for a Republican for president since 1988 but Trump somehow conveniently won them by approximately 44000, 22000 and 10000 votes respectively. All states he needed to win. Robert Mueller's investigation found plenty of contacts with Russians by the Trump campaign including the fact that Paul Manafort gave polling data to the Russians. Why would he do that? That is the textbook definition of collusion. The Russians needed to know where they needed to focus on to help trump win. Very suspicious!

TRADE

Donald Trump's trade policy has really hurt US farmers. His tariffs on Chinese goods have caused the Chinese to retaliate by imposing tariffs on exports to China. In other words, farmers now must pay a tax to export their produce that they did not have to pay before. Many soybean farmers in states like Iowa that voted for Trump in 2016 have been deeply affected by the trade war that Trump started. Many have filed for bankruptcy while others received a government bailout to sustain profitability. Rural America is in a recession right now.

China and other countries that use to buy soybeans and other products from American farmers are now looking at other markets around the world. What that means for soybean farmers is they may have permanently lost a big reliable market for their produce due to tariffs. That is going to hurt them for years and possibly generations to come and sadly many of them helped put Trump in office. Democrats would be wise to discuss a plan for these farmers.

Trump also withdrew from a trade deal, **Trans-Pacific Partnership (TPP)** that would have opened new markets to American Farmers and exporters. Twelve nations that negotiated the TPP were the U.S., Japan, Australia, Peru, Malaysia, Vietnam, New Zealand, Chile, Singapore, Canada, Mexico, and Brunei Darussalam. The harm that Trump has done to the American worker and Farmer is irreparable.

NGC Image: Countries that negotiated TPP

FOREIGN POLICY

Trump's foreign policy is a disaster. He has alienated our allies around the world and has sided with strong men and dictators. Our allies no longer trust or respect us, and our enemies no longer respect or fear us. Trump has failed at kissing the ass of Kim Jung un who is now firing missiles again. He does not respect the occupant of the white house.

Photo by By Gryphen|July 1st, 2019|Categories: Comics

Trump also withdrew America from the Iran nuclear deal which was negotiated by the Obama administration to prevent Iran from building a nuclear weapon. The Trump administration has slapped some sanctions on Iran and labeled the Iran Revolutionary Guard as a terrorist organization. Now that is a complete assault on Iran. It has forced Iran to lash out in the middle east by attacking oil tankers, shooting down a US drone and seizing British ships. We are closer to war with Iran today because of the idiotic behavior of this President whose sole purpose is destroying the legacy of President Obama without considering the consequences of his actions.

Everywhere Trump goes in the world, there are massive protests. He is an embarrassment of a president. He has made America's standing in the world much weaker than it was two and a half years ago.

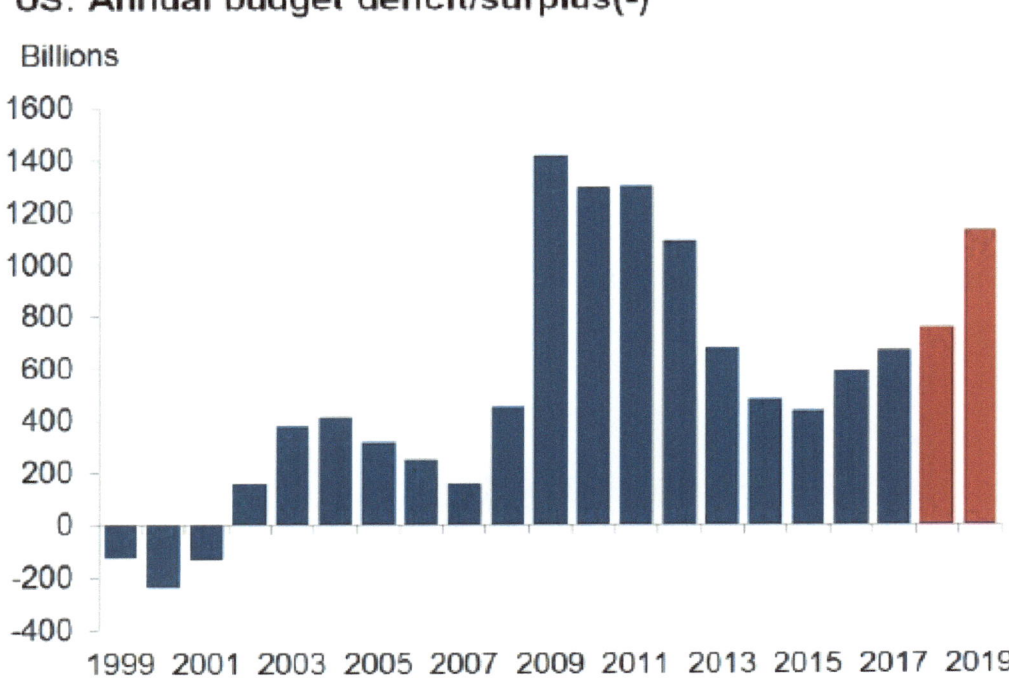

US: Annual budget deficit/surplus(-)

Source : Oxford Economics/US Treasury

Bush inherited a budget surplus of $280 billion from the Clinton administration. He doubled the debt by time he left office due to tax cuts, two unfunded wars and the creation of Medicare part D, all on the nations credit card. His policies of deregulation that let wall street operate without any checks and balances, led to the great recession. The end of his presidency, the 280 billion budget surplus he inherited had turn into a 1.2 trillion-dollar deficit which he passed on to Obama. Obama inherited an economy in free fall plus a massive deficit. An average of 500,000 jobs were being lost per month when he took office on January 2009.

In just 6 months in office, President Obama turned the economy around by passing an economic stimulus package opposed by Republicans, saving the auto industry and passing regulatory reforms. July 2019 marked 10 years of economic expansion. Obama was President for 7 ½ years of that but Trump likes to take credit for the economy like his policies are the reason. He can thank Obama for the economy.

Trump inherited a booming economy from Obama with a deficit cut in more than half. He was shameless enough to take credit for the job numbers in February 2017, just 1 month into his presidency. He has been taking credit since then despite job killing policies like government shutdowns, trade wars that have caused a socialist bailout of farmers, tax cuts (corporate welfare) that has exploded the deficit, the economy is still doing well. Thanks Obama!

The only credit trump gets is doubling the deficit during great economic times when deficits are supposed to fall. What happens if there is a recession?! It is a shame that this man that has a record of bankrupting several casinos and businesses he has owned is now doing the same to the country.

Deficits fall during good economic times or as the economy improves. Trump has turned an Obama economy build on solid fundamentals to an artificial economy bolstered by massive government spending to make up for bad policies like the trade war with China. A truly good economy would have the budget deficit falling not rising. Trump needs to be called out on this every time he takes credit for the economy; deficits are rising and far less jobs are being added now than under the last 3 years of Obama.

There is bound to be a recession soon and it most likely will destroy the financial stability of this country for generations to come.

Republican presidents have never been good for the U.S economy. Their only policy for the economy is cutting taxes which explodes the deficit. Democrats have to come in and clean the mess every time!

Trump promised to balance the budget and eliminate the national debt in 8 yrs. The budget deficit is projected to be about over a trillion dollars this year. Trump is going to add $3 trillion to the debt most likely before he has been in office for 3 years. The debt Trump is adding is not as a result of a recession and less people working like during Obama's 1st term. It is directly from Trump/Republican policies: Massive tax cuts from 35% to 21% for corporations, and a sizable increase in military and domestic spending. He is the biggest fraud that ever walked on the face of the earth, but his supporters do not care. If he continues his racism and he 'sticks it to the liberals', his base will continue to support him. In order to beat Trump, Democrats have to point out these facts about the economy, debt and deficits.

HOW TO UNIFY AMERICA

The two major political parties, Republicans and Democrats are so divided right now that even things that used to be done for the good of the country cannot even be brought up for a vote. Case in point, the 2013 Immigration bill which passed the senate with 68 votes was never brought to the house floor for a vote so essentially Jon Boehner killed that bill that would have prevented a lot of issues we see today at the border.

Mitch McConnell has also held up a gun control law bill which passed the house. He has not brought that up for a vote in the senate. He also refused to put on the floor an election security bill that passed the house to make sure that Russia and other bad actors do not have the ability to interfere in our elections.

Years ago, this would have easily been passed by both chambers. Not anymore. Even election security is now a partisan issue because 'Moscow' Mitch McConnell feels like passing that bill will prevent them from winning elections because he believes Trump and the Republicans cannot win without Russian help. There is no other explanation!

So, I have discussed most of the things that divide us as a country from guns to healthcare to taxes to immigration and things Democrats need to talk about to defeat Trump. With all these divisions, how can we unify our country?

The best way to unify America is to divide it in two temporarily: Republican America and Democrat America. Those that vote for

Republicans get to live exclusively under Republican orthodoxy which means you cannot continue to vote for Republicans and then continue to enjoy all the benefits that Democrats fight for.

Since Republicans are in court to take away healthcare, only Republicans healthcare should be taken away, only republicans Medicare, Medicaid and Social Security should get cut. Only republican's safety net programs should be cut. Only republicans that have abortions should go to jail. Let the corporations run everything. Only republican states can have an EPA that does not protect their environment. Since they are so anti socialism, they can repeal public education as well. Public education is the true definition of socialism. Homeowners often with no kids or with grown kids get taxed so other people's kids can go to school for free. Republicans would appreciate paying for their kids' education from K-12 instead of that free public socialist education that liberals force down their throats just like the free healthcare they want to give them. There will be no control on protecting the environment. No minimum wage. Because Republicans do not understand the function of taxes, they most likely will cut taxes to the point of insolvency which means not enough funds for the military, research and development, infrastructure.

Democrats will live in a country governed by Democrats which means they will not have Republicans blocking all their efforts. They will have their citizens on affordable or universal healthcare, they will live in a country with 21st century infrastructure, Medicare, Medicaid and Social Security will be fully funded, citizens will have affordable college and be free from gun violence due to gun reform laws Democrats will pass. There will be safety net programs that will make sure that when a citizen falls on hard times, they can maintain their dignity. The environment will the protected.

Blue states tend to be the wealthiest in the nation and some of the democrat policies are already working for Democrats in those states. I am confident that once the Republican base is no longer blinded by racism, and they have to live under all those cruel policies that their party puts forth without Democrat intervention, they will realize that the Democrat party is not as bad as they thought.

Just like Obamacare, once it was under threat to be repealed, most of the people that benefited from it but opposed it because of opposition to Obama, began to realize how good a deal they had. Democrats won big on healthcare in the 2018 midterms.

If Republicans were forced to live under their party's bad policies, in a few years, I can say with confidence that they would start voting for or at least be open to supporting Democrats.

Democrats most likely will not want to go back to living in situations where they would be denied those benefits that they have enjoyed. Remember, if it was left to conservatives, Medicare and Social Security would never have happened. Now they are the most popular entitlement programs in the country, and both are pure socialism!